THE STORY OF IRISH EMIGRATION

First published in 1999 by
Mercier Press
PO Box 5 5 French Church St Cork
Tel: (021) 275040; Fax: (021) 274969; e.mail: books@mercier.ie
16 Hume Street Dublin 2
Tel: (01) 661 5299; Fax: (01) 661 8583; e.mail: books@marino.ie

Trade enquiries to CMD Distribution 55A Spruce Avenue
Stillorgan Industrial Park Blackrock County Dublin
Tel: (01) 294 2556; Fax: (01) 294 2564

ISBN 1 85635 249 8
10 9 8 7 6 5 4 3 2 1

Cover painting reproduced with the kind permission of
the Trustees of the National Museums & Galleries of
Northern Ireland
Cover design by Penhouse Design
Printed in Ireland by ColourBooks Baldoyle Dublin 13

THE STORY OF IRISH EMIGRATION

FRANK D'ARCY

MERCIER PRESS

CONTENTS

FOREWORD

A particular feature of the late twentieth century which has occupied the minds of governments and continues to arouse dissension and pity among ordinary citizens is the great flood of migrants and refugees in so many parts of the world. Yet this great movement and displacement of people is no entirely new development, and the history of one small island provides a striking example of exile and opportunity, of disaster and welcome, of hardship and faithful memory.

This short account attempts to provide an impression of this long-lasting movement of people which in recent centuries has involved so many men and women not only in Great Britain and other parts of Europe, but in North America, Australasia and beyond. It is hoped that this story and the issues of dislocation and assimilation – and even transformation – which it raises will not be without relevance to the problems of migrants and refugees so evident in the contemporary world.

Such an account could not be attempted

without drawing on the work of many scholars and chroniclers and some effort is made to acknowledge the debt in the Further Reading section at the end of the work. Another kind of acknowledgement is due to Mr Sean McMahon whose support was indispensabie, to the staff at the library in Magee College, Derry, and to Ms Jo O'Donoghue for her initiative and patience, and very particularly to some others closer to home who might have wondered if some kind of internal migration was taking place but who never once complained.

1

SCOTTI ET SANCTI

Who were the first people to leave the shores of Ireland as emigrants? This is so complicated a question that it is better not to be delayed here by proposing an answer. It is clearly possible to know a good deal about the people who lived in Ireland thousands of years ago from the evidence they left behind them concerning their diet, their weapons, their homes, their tools and their tombs. All these can be explored using the techniques of modern archaeology and relevant scientific disciplines. Yet it is only after our distant ancestors began to leave behind them deliberate records, whether in written language or in oral tradition much later written down, that it becomes possible to get a more comprehensive idea of who they were and what they were actually thinking.

Scholars have found it difficult to be certain about who the various peoples were who came and settled in Ireland in the many centuries before the Christian era. Certainly there must have been departures as well as arrivals, but we can begin the story of Irish emigration not earlier than the fifth century AD when it is clear that two broad movements had been taking place. People from the north-east of Ireland were moving across to what is now western Scotland and at about the same period other people from the east and south-east of Ireland were crossing to what is now western Wales.

This movement of people, particularly to Scotland, remains an episode of outstanding interest, even though it happened so long ago, for its consequences have remained visible virtually up to our own time. It has been a peculiarity of the long history of emigration from Ireland that the emigrants never trans-planted to any real extent the Irish or Gaelic language into any of the many places in which they settled. The one exception is the settlement in nearby Scotland where the Gaelic language first flourished in the west, then gradually spread to districts of the north and east.

Even the name of Scotland arises from this early migration, for the Romans had given the name of Scoti or Scotti to the Gaelic-speaking Irish, and for many centuries the island of Ireland was widely known as Scotia. Thus the people who moved over to the neighbouring island were known as Scoti and as time went on and the influence of these Scoti in their new home grew, their name was applied to all the people of the territory. By about the eleventh century the terms Scot and Scotia were applied exclusively to Scotland and no longer to Ireland. This happened despite the fact that the Scoti were only one of the peoples present in Scotland in those centuries.

It is difficult to estimate the numbers of people who went over to the island of Britain or the numbers of their descendants, but we have definite information about various out-standing individuals. The most dramatic thing that had happened to Ireland in those centuries was its embracing of Christianity and the adoption at least by a minority of a dedicated Christian way of life. One consequence was the flow outwards of monks and priests, some to Britain, some to the continent of Europe and some to scattered islands of the north, to the Faroes and even to Iceland. A truly distinguished figure amongst them was the monk Colmcille, or Columba, who crossed to what is now the Western Isles of Scotland about the year 563 and went on to establish on the small island of Iona, off Mull, a monastery that can be said, without empty exaggeration, to have played a notable part in the history of Ireland, Scotland and even England itself.

We know about Columba because about a hundred years after his death a successor of his as abbot of Iona, Adamnan by name, wrote an account of him which was a work of celebration and piety rather than a strict biography, but which contained much invaluable information. Columba's existence and the result of his life's work was also known to the great English monk and writer, Bede of Northumbria; and so deep was Columba's impact and that of the monasteries he inspired that a whole tradition of legend and poetry about him grew up in Ireland itself. One of the continuing themes of this poetry was that of exile from the beloved land of Ireland, a theme of recollection with sadness that was to recur in the history of Irish emigration many centuries later.

One of the stories which Adamnan relates about Columba offers a provoking insight into the mentality of these clerical migrants. The story may be a reasonably authentic account of an incident in Columba's life or, at the very least, reflect the mind of Adamnan, Columba's later successor. It tells of the robber Erc who used to make off with seals which the monks regarded as their property. During the day Erc used to hide on the island of Mull, turning his boat upside down and covering it with grass, and then sail off at night to the breeding ground of the seals. He was taken hold of by two of the monks and brought to Columba who scolded him for stealing what belonged to others. But then, probably to Erc's surprise, the abbot added that if he was in need, he should come to the monks and be given what he required.

To round off the story, Adamnan says that Columba later foresaw that Erc was at the point of death and arranged that a quantity of food be sent off to him as a last gift. It arrived on the day of his death and, as a final touch, it was used at his funeral. Hardly a bedtime story for advocates of zero tolerance.

Life for these monks was not all sweetness and light. People came, even Saxons, to live and study among them and this must have contributed to the famous mission of Aidan and other Gaelic-speaking monks to Northumbria and other parts of England. These men were highly praised by the Anglo-Saxon Bede for their Christian influence and integrity, and he recorded for history the names and work of Aidan, Finan and Colman and of the pupils of Celtic monasteries such as Cuthbert and Chad. The leading role of the Gaels themselves was doubtless ended at the synod of Whitby in 664 when a famous decision was taken not to accept some of their distinctive practices, such as a method of calculating the date of Easter and a way of arranging the clerical tonsure. The connection between Ireland and Northumbria was not entirely broken, however, and continued in interesting ways. These monks were migrants with a message, and while it would be misleading to say that there were great numbers of them, their message was appreciated and their impact important.

It was not only to Britain and the northern isles that these early Scoti sailed. Their migration was not like the outflow from Ireland in later centuries, for the people about whom we have reasonably reliable information were monks, clergy and scholars, a select enough section of the population in any era. It obviously requires some explanation to account for their presence to some degree in what are now Belgium, France, Germany, Austria, Switzerland and Italy. One element in the situation, not the greatest but surely ironic, was the Latin language.

Ireland was unusual in western Europe in that the Romans had never invaded it and thus it had never become part of the Roman Empire through which Latin spread. Christianity was another matter, however, for the Irish strongly embraced it and with it its language of solemn worship, church business and scholarship. This Latin language had to be learned by the Gaelic-speaking clergy for their official ceremonies and prayers, for the psalm and gospel books they were copying and for communication with churches in other countries. They became quite famous for their interest in Latin grammar and its texts.

Three phases of this movement to the continent can be discerned. A younger contemporary of Colmcille's spent many years in Ireland before leaving the monastery of Bangor about the year 590, on his way to set in motion a remarkable train of events in several lands of the former Roman Empire. This monk, Columbanus, set up a monastery in Luxeuil in what is now eastern France and the rule of life that he established there, ascetic and penitential as it undoubtedly was, was taken up vigorously by his Frankish followers. The great Canadian scholar, James Kenney, once wrote that so many founders of religious houses in seventh-century Gaul drew their inspiration from Luxeuil that the later writers of saints' lives of the period just assigned almost everyone to the monastery founded by Columbanus.

The pilgrim abbot was not slow to speak his mind. We are fortunate that a number of his well-written letters in Latin have been preserved, in which he defends the customs of the Irish church or gives advice to the Pope, or reminds the local bishops that 'we are all members together of one body, whether Gauls or Britons or Irish (Iberi) or any other race.' His criticisms of local rulers very nearly led to his ejection from the continent, but he managed to go instead on an extraordinary journey from Nantes to the edge of Normandy, and then right across to Koblenz on the Rhine. With his companion from Bangor, the monk Gall, he continued downwards to the borders of modern Austria and Switzerland, staying for some time at Bregenz on Lake Constance. His final move was to cross over to what is now Italy and found the last of his monasteries at Bobbio, where he died in 613.

Columbanus was not the only pilgrim monk of that century. His companion Gall established a hermitage which later became the great monastery of St Gallen in Switzerland. Another exile, Fursey, or Fursa, is recorded enthusiastically for posterity by the writer Bede, who tells of the famous vision attributed to that monk and of his setting up a monastery near Yarmouth in south-eastern England before leaving for France about the year 644. Upon his death a few years later, Fursey's body was brought to a church at Peronne, a town that was later known as Peronne of the Scotti.

A striking number of other pious men and women of the period were described as Scotti or Irish but the historical records relating to them are so scanty or dubious that the legends can very often not be verified. We have grounds to accept that one Goban, a follower of Fursey, did exist, and we certainly know that a St Gobain gave his name to a forest famous in French history and to a village near Laon. There is also a long tradition about the missionary Kilian who was killed at Wurzburg in Germany about 689, a tradition that still survives, but in his case we have to rely on slim and scattered pieces of evidence. The same may be said more forcefully of St Dympna of Gheel near Antwerp in Belgium. She is still remembered as the patroness of those suffering from insanity and her legend describes her as Irish, but no reliable contemporary records have survived to separate legend from fact.

The strangest case of all may be that of

Fiacre, still recalled today as the patron of gardeners and even of taxi drivers. The earliest surviving account of his life was written some 500 years after he died. Yet shrines in his honour remain surprisingly abundant in the Paris region, and the horse-drawn carriage of the seventeenth century, the fiacre, drew its name from the Paris church dedicated to him. The record has disappeared, while the tradition and legend remain. Over many parts of France, Germany and Belgium, indeed, there are shrines or place names recalling men and women whom tradition claimed as coming from Ireland: St Wendel in the Saarland, Landelin in Alsace, Saint Saens in Normandy or Fridolin of Sackingen. A good many may be like Cathaldus of Tarentum in Italy who was given an Irish origin that was evidently fictitious. The modern traveller may be surprised to find so many traces but should not be too easily persuaded by them.

There was a second wave of expatriates from Ireland beginning about the year 800 and the more prominent among these are remembered as scholars rather than saints. This was the period when the attacks and settlement of the

Norsemen in Ireland were taking effect, and it may be no coincidence that many references start appearing to an Irish presence in the new empire created by the Frankish leader, Charlemagne. The comment of one writer of the time has often been recalled: Waalfrid Strabo who seemed to have had various contacts with the Irish, wrote that they were a people 'with whom the custom of travelling into foreign lands has now almost become second nature.'

Another writer went even further. Heiric of Auxerre wrote, 'Why should I mention Ireland, of which almost the whole people, scorning the dangers of the sea, migrate with their crowd of philosophers to our shore?' These observers were not statisticians and the total number of migrants could not have been huge, but the incomers were clearly making their presence felt in the schools and monasteries of Charlemagne's Europe.

The two best-remembered figures among this group are among the great enigmas of Irish history. By the titles given to them and other evidence we know that Sedulius Scottus the poet and John Scottus (Eriugena) the philosopher were Scotti or Irish.

The philosophical texts of John Scottus are part of the history of European philosophy: his biblical and other commentaries still engage the attention of scholars. But where exactly he was born and from what family and who were his teachers, we just do not know. He wrote in Latin and was noted for his knowledge of Greek but alas no real account of his life was written at the time or at least not preserved. He was active at Laon in France between about 845 and 870, but we do not even know when he died.

Sedulius Scottus, his contemporary, was an accomplished and witty poet, and scholars attribute to him the authorship of a variety of texts, theological and political. He was one of a group of Irish scribes and scholars at Liege in Belgium, arriving there about 848. The English scholar, Robin Flower, concluded that he came from Leinster, but there is much that we do not know about this fascinating pilgrim scholar.

Nor were these two alone. Charlemagne had been eager to advance education and learning in his empire and the leading figure in this campaign was clearly the English monk Alcuin from York. But prominent in the palace school was Clemens Scottus whose surviving writings mostly concern grammar. There was Dicuil who wrote a long astronomical poem and a book of geography which contains some fascinating pieces of information from other wandering Scotti. There seems to have been more than one Dungal, and Josephus Scottus the friend of Alcuin is thought to be the same Josephus of whose Latin poems several survive.

Yet just as intriguing are the anonymous scribes and annotators who wrote poems and comments in Old Irish on the margins of manuscripts still surviving in continental libraries. From these, modern scholars, beginning with the great German Johann Zeuss, were able to construct a grammar and systematic understanding of Old Irish. Other anonymous monks and scholars wrote biblical commentaries and there are still disputes, as in the case of illuminated manuscripts, as to whether certain works were written by Anglo-Saxon or by Irish writers. It is not for nothing that a Swiss scholar wrote in 1956 an article entitled 'Iromanie - Irophobie', a title which neatly suggests that there existed a band of scholars passionately emphasising Irish achievements, while another group was sceptical or hostile to such claims.

A third phase of this early medieval contact with the continent was less dramatic and probably on a lesser scale. It resulted in the establishment in Germany mainly from about 1000 to 1200 of a series of monasteries, later known as Schotten-kloster, in such centres as Ratisbon (Reichenau), Wurzburg, Vienna, Nuremberg and elsewhere. Irish monks were certainly present in these centres and it is curious that the two most famous were both from Ulster and had the same name, Marianus Scottus. One of these was from the MacRoarty family of Donegal. As time went on, the Irish faded out of these monasteries and at a much later date Ratisbon, for example, was handed over to Scottish ecclesiastics.

The story of this early Irish movement into Europe is a long one stretching over 500 years. Its most prominent features were ecclesiastical and its participants were evidently mostly male and by no means always saintly. The records are not short of rows, criticisms and the occasional denunciation. But many aspects of it were remarkable and do not lose their fascination for a modern mind.

Emigration from Ireland did not, of course, come to a complete stop at this point of the early Middle Ages but new situations were arising. It was immigration that was becoming an increasing force in Irish life, beginning with the Norse and Danish settlements notably in Dublin, Waterford and other city-ports. At the end of the twelfth century began the Anglo-Norman invasion which was to have such long-lasting and formative effects on the island's development. Irish people could certainly be found leaving the island as soldiers whether in Scottish wars or with the Black Prince at Crecy in France in the fourteenth century or later with Henry V at Agincourt. Stray vagrants turn up in critical English records, and boisterous scholars at Oxford, or pilgrims to Rome or Compostella. But there does not seem to have been any great movement of people, and evidently none that has been carefully recorded. Ireland of the high medieval period had its wars, its plagues, its churches and castles, and its personalities, but no great exodus of people. It was a calm before the storm.

2

MERCENARIES AND WILD GEESE

A thousand years of history lay between the
departure of Columba for Iona and the declaration in 1541 that King Henry VIII of
England was no longer merely Lord of Ireland
but its king as well. In those intervening centuries
new people had settled into the island, Scan-
dinavian and English, Norman and Scots and
Welsh, and the English language took root in
various eastern areas and in walled towns around
the island. Powerful lords of Norman and English
origin conquered large stretches of territory and
ruled there, sometimes on good terms with
neighbouring Gaelic chiefs and sometimes de-
cidedly not.

As time went on, many of these Anglo-
Normans settled more deeply into Irish life,
following Gaelic customs and speaking the Irish

language. While proud of their origins and status, they occasionally married Irish wives and maintained poets to compose Gaelic verse to their honour and glory. This process was not, however, as complete as some writers have argued. The English king kept his representative in Ireland, and a considerable area around Dublin often described as the English Pale was governed under English law, and its leading people distinguished themselves from the 'mere Irish'.

A similar state of affairs could be found in cities like Waterford, Limerick and Galway where leading family names were unlikely to begin with O or Mac but rather to be simply Lombard or Woulfe, French or Bodkin. Iron-ically, in the light of what happened later, the part of the country least under Anglo-Norman control was the province of Ulster where, in large part, Gaelic lords such as O'Neill and O'Donnell ruled according to traditional laws and customs. They guarded their privileges jealously against Norman and English intruders, Gaelic neigh-bours and each other.

This coexistence of cultures has to be kept in mind when one tries to understand the migrations from Ireland in the seventeenth and eighteenth centuries. The Ireland that was emerging from the Middle Ages endured much division in the form of tribal raids between Gaelic chiefs themselves, in battles between those chiefs and the English king's representative and in conflicts of an even more complicated nature. But there were also interests that linked together the inhabitants of the island. The Irish of that period, whatever their origins or indeed their behaviour, were to show a notable attachment to the traditional organisation of the Christian Church. The Gaels and the Anglo-Norman Irish may have quarrelled savagely about territory and lifestyle and about relationships with England, but in matters of religion they followed the same liturgy and accepted the same doctrines.

Scholars today argue about why this happened and what was really involved, but two momentous developments outside Ireland were to bring about a crisis which was to envelop both Gael and Anglo-Norman alike. The existing practices and doctrinal interpretations of Western Christendom were challenged in the 1500s in the movement known as the Reformation, and gradually most of Europe split into two areas – those where the Reformed faiths were fostered and those where the old or Catholic Church was dominant. In most of northern Europe it was the Reformed faith, in various forms, that prevailed.

The second momentous development was the outward movement of European peoples, the urge to colonise the New World or the Indies and even what were seen as the less modernised parts of Europe itself. It was Ireland's fate that the desire of the Tudor kings to strengthen their hold over the whole country, together with the conflict over religion within Europe and the eager interest of the English to create new colonies, including some close to home, all came together to change the face of the island. One consequence was the start of a flow of people out of Ireland that was to continue for almost four hundred years and to be one of the most distinctive features of its history.

The first signs of what was to come can be seen in the wars between the lords of the southern province of Munster and the English

Tudor rulers. In the latter half of the sixteenth
century, the English introduced colonies of
settlers into the midlands and Munster and
started to impose on Ireland the ecclesiastical
changes and doctrines already established in
England. Irish soldiers had already begun to
serve in the Spanish army, and Irish leaders,
stressing their loyalty to the traditional Catholic
faith, were looking to Spain for military aid.
Among the English in Munster were two men
later legendary in the literature of English –
Edmund Spenser and Walter Raleigh. But for
the Irish, these Desmond campaigns in the
south and Lord Baltinglass's revolt in Leinster
and, above all, the Nine Years War conducted
mainly by the Ulster chiefs, Hugh O'Neill and
Hugh O'Donnell, brought not only defeat and
desolation but the departure of contingents of
soldiers for continental armies.

The English, eager to be rid of possible
troublemakers, shipped soldiers out of Ulster,
later drawing bitter words from the exiled Hugh
O'Neill who had himself fled the country in
1607. He had been sent out of the way to Rome
but he denounced what he saw as the dispatching

of his former soldiers 'to the armies of foreign heretic kingdoms.' He mentioned in particular the sending of 1,200 soldiers to serve the King of Sweden against the King of Poland. 'Now,' he said, 'like another race of gypsies they wander through the world, lost.'

For the rest of that century, continental states were eager to recruit Irish soldiers to fill gaps in their expanding armies. The dynastic and religious wars that were plaguing Europe created a demand for men who could face the hardship, disease and dangers of the military life. More than one continental observer commented on the endurance and physical agility of Irish soldiers, and one colonel of an Irish regiment claimed that on a journey by horseback from Chalons to Paris he was followed by an Irish servant on foot – who always managed to arrive to take the reins when it was time to change horses.

Some modern historians, in fact, reacting against romantic pictures of patriotic men persecuted for their religious beliefs and driven out of their own country, have presented these soldiers simply as mercenaries, hired as battle fodder by warring monarchies and only too often meeting an early and miserable end. Certainly Europe was full of mercenaries and of demand for mercenaries, and many young men must have considered a career as a mercenary in France or Spain as a better prospect than life as the defeated party in Ireland. But that was not the whole story. The old leaders and elite in Ireland had progressively been dispossessed, and the old religion discouraged and, at intervals, undeniably persecuted. And it is likely that some departing exiles retained the idea that the Irish conflict had not been finally resolved, and that a departing soldier could yet find a reason to return.

The numbers that left Ireland for the continent in the seventeenth and eighteenth centuries were not great by later standards, and neither is it easy to decide from the existing records how many soldiers were involved at a particular time. The historian Louis Cullen has offered a broad estimate that up to 60,000 men left Ireland for continental service in the 1600s and that some dependants, fewer in number, accompanied them. Estimates made by some other historians of various phases of the movement would tend to support this figure, but from the nature of the case – and the nature of the records – certainty is not easily attained.

The situation is clearer when one looks at the peak moments of departure. After the defeat of the northern earls in the early 1600s, a tradition of Irish regiments in the Spanish service was established which continued with little interruption for 200 years. There were several Irish regiments in Spanish Flanders in the seventeenth century under colonels such as Owen Roe O'Neill and Thomas Preston. When an English viceroy enrolled an army in Ireland with many Catholics in it in the late 1630s, and then had to disband it under pressure from the English parliament, Spain was more than eager to recruit large numbers from it, but this proved very difficult. And then when a long and complicated Irish war came to an end with a Cromwellian victory and a crushing settlement, there was a mass exodus of the soldiers of the defeated armies.

The surprisingly large figure of between 30,000 and 35,000 departing soldiers is accepted by many historians, and there are harrowing accounts of harsh sea voyages, attacks of plague and hardships on arrival. Many of the soldiers went to Spain and others ended up in the French army, and there were changes of allegiance and desertions. A dozen regiments appeared in the Spanish service, some briefly or suffering quick amalgamation while others, like those of Colonels Morphy, O'Meara or O'Reilly, were relatively long lasting.

Regiments were also formed in the French service, eight at one time under Colonels Butler, McCarthy and others, but these were quickly reduced in number. A complication was that the Irish most loyal to Charles II, who was himself an exile in France, had moved there to support him, some even abandoning Spain. This loyalty to the Stuart king was more typical of the Old Anglo-Norman Irish than of the Gaelic Irish, but intermarriage, shared interests and hardships were bringing the two parties closer together, and many Gaelic names are found among Charles's supporters.

When Charles was restored to the throne of England, many of the Irish hoped that their days of exile were over and not a few of those who had had estates looked forward to regaining them, but there was much bitter disappointment ahead. The restored king, aware of the influence of his former Cromwellian and parliamentary enemies, did not risk changing the whole Cromwellian settlement in Ireland and giving back to his Irish followers their former estates. A number were restored but the regime in Ireland was fearful of giving power and influence to Catholics.

Then came a turn of events which would have seemed amazing to those who had sailed away from Ireland in 1653. Charles died, and his brother James who succeeded him as King was a Catholic who duly appointed an Irishman, Richard Talbot, as his Lord Deputy in Ireland. This Talbot began quickly to change the power base in the country, replacing the army which was almost wholly Protestant in character by one that was very largely Catholic and preparing the way for a parliament that would be composed predominantly of Catholic members. But there was strong opposition in England to King James, and in 1688 he was ousted and replaced by

William of Orange and Queen Mary. The result for Ireland was another bitter war lasting for the best part of three years and which placed in Irish memory names that have only been too well remembered – the Siege of Derry, the Battle of the Boyne and the Treaty of Limerick.

The war ended late in 1691 with victory for the Williamite army and with the departure once again of thousands of Irish soldiers for Europe. This time the destination was France and there is again some difficulty in discovering the exact number of men who sailed, for they were taken in both French and British ships, and there were some confusing reports. Several regiments had gone over earlier in the war and there were some other departures, but taking all these together, and not including dependants, a figure of up to 20,000 seems realistic. Those who went at the end of the war did not have an easy landing in France, for some were ill and others were found unsuitable. They formed what was a Jacobite army in French pay, but many officers found they had to accept a lower rank than that which they held in Ireland.

The situation for the Irish on the continent

was not quite the same in the 1690s as it had been a century earlier. Two other categories of person had gone overseas in the intervening years, of which the most visible was the clergy. Stricter arrangements for the education of the Catholic clergy together with laws in Ireland that restricted Catholic schools, had the result that what could not be done in Ireland had to be done outside it. Thus a whole series of colleges and seminaries was established across the continent. One was founded in Salamanca in 1592 and there were four others in Spain. A cluster of them grew up in the Spanish Netherlands, at Douai in 1594 and Louvain in 1624, the first of three at that university city, and at Antwerp.

Perhaps the most famous was the Irish College at Paris which began to take a fixed shape about 1605 and moved its location several times until its present site in the Rue des Irlandais. There were at various times eight other colleges in France of which the largest was at Nantes, which started in 1680. The others were at university cities such as Rouen, Bordeaux and Toulouse. Some colleges were further away, such as a small institution at Lisbon and a quite substantial Franciscan college at Prague; and in the city of Rome three colleges from the period are still in existence today, each of them with a remarkable history – the Irish College notable for the distinguished ecclesiastics who emerged from it, the Dominican priory of San Clemente with the famous archaeological remains that lie beneath it, and the Franciscan college of St Isidore's founded by Luke Wadding in 1625 and notable both for its history and its furnishings.

It has to be stressed that these colleges were founded for the education of the clergy who were expected to return to Ireland whether as parish clergy or members of religious orders. Many were small, poor and austere, and several experienced unedifying disputes about who should be admitted to them or who should control them. But they also provided a base for what remained of the intelligentsia of the older Ireland. Some of the staff were professors at the local universities and some wrote books of theology, doctrine or history, often in Latin and sometimes in Irish or English. The study of the early Irish church was a topic of especial interest both for writers of old Anglo-Irish background and for those from Gaelic families. They could boast some distinguished scholars such as the Franciscans Luke Wadding, Florence Conry and John Colgan or others such as Michael Moore at Paris.

These colleges also carried out other functions. They were outposts which reminded their continental neighbours of the existence of Ireland. They were fixed centres where wandering soldiers or traders knew that they could find fellow countrymen. Older exiles occasionally remembered them in their wills, and in some of them students did not carry on to priestly ordination but turned to the army or some other profession. For the most part, their role came to an end at the close of the eighteenth century when it became possible to maintain Catholic colleges and seminaries in Ireland. A few continued on as seminaries right up to the twentieth century but the buildings at Paris and Louvain are today devoted to more diverse activities.

The number of clergy and students present in these institutions at any one time was not great by modern standards. The historian Cathaldus Giblin estimated the total number as approximately 600 around the year 1780. These were not the only Irish clergy in France for it was a constant complaint that quite a number did not go home but took up parish work or other work on the continent. The names of a considerable number of priests who acted as chaplains in the French and Spanish forces have also been recorded. The situation varied, of course, with the conditions in Ireland, particularly the vigour with which the government enforced laws banishing bishops and members of religious orders. The government in Ireland accused the friars in particular of encouraging sedition and foreign interference, and this was more of a preoccupation at periods in the first half of the eighteenth century than in the second.

The bishops and priests were, of course, men but there were also some Irishwomen who spent their lives as nuns in continental convents. Their numbers seem comparatively small and they were scattered in various convents especially in France and Flanders. Perhaps only two houses were described as specifically Irish – a convent at Ypres in Flanders and another in Lisbon. Women were clearly a minority in the emigration to the continent in these centuries and this was as true of the wives and single women who departed with or followed the armies as it was of the women in religious life.

The presence of a considerable number of educated Irish clergy abroad could not have failed to have some effect on the course of events in Ireland. They were in a position to give a view of the Irish situation to interested observers on the continent that was different from that of the Irish authorities and British diplomats. The flow of secular clergy who returned to Ireland from the colleges must have brought some awareness of a wider world and other traditions than those now dominant at home.

Yet it was the soldiers rather than the clergy who mostly attracted the attention of both the British and continental authorities. The Irish Jacobite army that went with Sarsfield to France found itself in the middle of a war which cost it many lives and much hardship. And at its conclusion in 1698, many of the veterans were simply disbanded and left to fend for themselves. Not a few wandered across Europe and found military service in the German states or Russia or for the emperor in Vienna.

It was not that France did not value Irish troops, for it now maintained a constant number of regiments in its own service even in peace time. For much of the eighteenth century there were six or seven such regiments, and three still existed at the time of the French revolution.

In Spain too, a whole new set of Irish regiments came into being in the early part of the eighteenth century. As time went on, these were reduced to three with the titles of Irlanda, Hibernia and Ultonia and they remained in existence until after the Napoleonic Wars, which ended in 1815. The Emperor in Vienna, usually an ally of England, gave many opportunities to Irish officers, although there was no tradition in the Austrian army of specifically Irish regiments. Louis Cullen has calculated that at any time in this century the French and Spanish armies offered about 500 commissions as officers to Irishmen, and opportunities were available in other services. The Irish soldier, at various levels of command, was a common enough figure in that war-strewn century.

The officers were recruited from Ireland, commonly from the sons of the remaining Irish Catholic gentry or former gentry, but also from the French- or Spanish-born sons of serving officers. Some family names such as those of the O'Neills, the Dillons, the Walls and the O'Donnells kept reappearing for generations. It was more difficult to arrange for a constant supply of ordinary soldiers to join foreign armies that might prove hostile to England. After the three major wars ending within Ireland in the 1600s, it seemed politic for the victorious government to move large numbers of the defeated armies overseas. In this way many thousands of ordinary soldiers left the country, but after that there were greater problems in getting recruits out to the continent.

From time to time recruiting officers were discovered in Ireland and executed. Many young men smuggled themselves out by boat or made their way across England and enlisted in Flemish or French ports. Another occasional source was from Irish-born soldiers in the English army who either deserted or joined the French army after capture. Irish Catholics were not supposed to be in the English army at that time but clearly some were, in spite of occasional warnings that this could be a dangerous policy. Recruits certainly arrived in France as one can see in various records such as the memoir of a veteran officer of the regiment of Dillon in 1739 who notes that 800 men had come from Ireland to the regiment in Sedan. Likewise, lists of troopers in a Franco-Irish cavalry regiment in the 1740s show a high proportion of men born in Ireland. Louis Cullen again has estimated that about 35,000 men went over to continental forces in the first half of the eighteenth century, not counting the flow of officers. Some contemporary voices on the continent put the figure as considerably higher, but clearly there have been some exaggerations.

An important characteristic of many of these emigré soldiers was their Jacobite loyalty; that is, their support of the deposed James II and of his son, described by the new regime in England as the Old Pretender but known to the Irish exiles as James III. It is sometimes forgotten that there were no fewer than six attempts between 1692 and 1759 to send troops to Britain from France and one attempt from Spain, and in all of these Irish exiles were involved, sometimes in a prominent way. This was particularly so of the independent effort of 'Bonnie Prince Charlie' in 1745 and of the projected French invasion of 1746 – and of an earlier repulse at La Hogue in 1692.

All these attempts except the last in 1759 were linked to the hope of a Jacobite restoration but they were foiled mainly by English naval power and a lack of real enthusiasm in England for a return of this royal family. The attempts, however, were a clear sign that many influential Irish exiles did not intend their stay on the continent to be final and permanent. The famous campaign of Bonnie Prince Charles in 1745–46 with its tragic consequences for Scotland was a reminder of another strand in the Irish emigration of the period – the presence of a ring of trading and merchant families in ports from Dunkirk to Cadiz and even to the Canary Islands. These were often sprung from merchant families who came under pressure in the coastal cities of Ireland and had set up business in France and Spain. It was men with such names as Hegarty, Walsh and Butler who were able to provide the means for Charles Edward Stuart to set off for Scotland in 1745 and to escape from it after his defeat. Other merchants were engaged in less dramatic business in Nantes or Bordeaux, and while their numbers were never great, they formed an interesting component of the continental emigration.

To generalise about this whole movement from 1600 to 1800 is not easy. It was born out of bitter times in Ireland and the numbers involved were substantial but not huge. One estimate for the two centuries is of about 150,000 persons, and it may be fewer than this. To this total must be added, of course, some of the descendants of the emigrants who maintained an Irish identity. The movement was linked to complications and differences about religion which were important to many of the participants. It has been argued this was particularly an emigration of an elite from Ireland, a departure of people who had high status in their own country, and there are some grounds for this. States such as Spain and the Austrian empire and, in some ways France, were willing to admit Irish exiles to high military rank and social position. The eighteenth century was one for Irish generals – Lacys, Brownes, Dillons, O'Neills and O'Donnells in profusion, Wall and O'Reilly. There was often an unseemly rush for Irish emigrants to prove their aristocratic origins, and there were some marriages into influential continental families. Many of the exiles had come from old Anglo-Irish backgrounds rather than purely Gaelic, but they often described themselves as of the Irish nation, and in fact the two traditions were closely bound together, intermarriage being common.

Yet most of the Irish were neither colonels nor lords, and the condition of their lives must often have been harsh. They created no sizeable colonies which would endure with their own special character for generations. Apart from the aristocracy, even their names seemed to fade away or be so transformed that only a specialist could identify them. Only a minority were women and thus the menfolk either remained unmarried or found wives who made it easier for them and their offspring to be absorbed into their host communities. Yet they certainly did not pass without leaving a mark. Their very existence was a threat to some in Ireland and a hope and encouragement to others. Their continuing interest in the fate of their homeland and their recurrent efforts to change the course of its politics puts one in mind of the later concern shown by many Irish-Americans for the political problems of Ireland. Indeed as the eighteenth century proceeded, it was not to continental Europe but to neighbouring England and, above all, to North America that Irish emigrants were now making their way.

3

BOUND FOR AMERIKAY

In 1537 a ship from Waterford set out across the Atlantic in the direction of the Newfoundland fisheries, undoubtedly one of the very first of a long line to make the voyage from that port. It is highly likely that even before then Irishmen had crossed that wide ocean, whether towards the cold northern lands being explored by the English or towards the warmer southern mainland and islands already claimed by Spain. These men were forerunners of many millions of Irish people who, together with other Europeans, sailed to seek a new life in what was for them a New World.

This movement was not just a case of a few hardy pioneers stumbling on a great opportunity and showing the way to millions of later migrants. Behind the great exodus lay a number of developments in European society. There was, for a start, the emergence of better technology in ships and weaponry, and the ambition of some more organised European states to increase their power and sources of wealth. Then there was the pressure of a gradually increasing population at home as more control of disease and epidemics was being attained; and often there was much discontent caused by economic hardship or by war and internal division.

Suddenly there came in sight the possibility of acquiring land and forms of wealth on a scale not possible in a crowded Europe. It was land, moreover, often sparsely populated by peoples whose technology and organisation of defence was no match for that developed by the Europeans. And it was within this general context of European expansion abroad that Irish migration to the Americas took place.

The early history of this migration is not easy to relate for some parts of it were never properly recorded, other records were lost and some have not yet been fully investigated. The first region of the Americas in which there seems to have been substantial immigration from Ireland was, perhaps surprisingly for the modern reader, the West Indies. Very early on, individual Irishmen are known to have been active on the South American mainland and in the islands, but it is from the 1630s onwards that considerable numbers of Irish are reported in the Carribean. They had gone there or been sent there as servants in various colonial projects planned from London or from within Ireland itself. It is now realised that some people involved in plantations and settlements in Ireland were also interested in projects in the Americas, and ships that went from Ireland carried people with them. Ireland also became a leading supplier of food and provisions to the West Indies, and this led some merchant families from ports such as Galway and Cork to become involved in plantations and send sons out there to work in business and other careers.

The upshot was that by the early 1640s considerable numbers of Irish were reported in islands such as Montserrat and St Kitts. A Jesuit priest stated in 1643 that a petition had been received from 20,000 Irish Catholics in St Kitts and neighbouring places, but that figure is certainly hard to believe. A few years later another reports speaks of 6,000 on St Kitts and Montserrat, and one can at least conclude that there were considerable numbers there, mostly working on plantations and many having come as indentured servants, i.e. working often under harsh contracts and harsh conditions. They were soon to be joined by another wave of migrants from Ireland, for one of the consequences of the Cromwellian conquest was the deportation of boatloads of men, women and boys in the early 1650s to the West Indies and particularly to Barbados. Again it is difficult to know the exact numbers involved, and there have been some exaggerations, but the respected historian Patrick Corish has proposed a figure of 12,000.

The death rate in the climate and conditions must have been high, and Catholics in the English colonies were at various times under suspicion and facing disabilities. An Irish priest, Dr Burgatt, wrote to Rome in 1666 claiming there was no priest there for 20,000 people but his figure may really have been a guess. A report twelve years later said that there were about 3,500 Irish on four islands including Antigua and Montserrat. Certainly the numbers of Irish dwindled and it is known that many white settlers moved away from the West Indies to the Carolinas and other colonies on the mainland, but according to David Doyle, there is virtually no evidence of the Irish being involved. The savage policy of enslaving Africans to work in the Carribean plantations was setting the future course of history in the islands. It is possible that there was some intermarriage between Irish and African workers and that their descendants became absorbed into the majority population.

It is fair to conclude that the fate of very many of the Irish who went or who were transported to the West Indies could not have been an easy one, but many questions about their history remain to be answered. The majority of these migrants shared in the manual labour of the fields or in associated work, but they were not the only Irish present in the islands. Among planters and traders can be found the names of Kirwan, Lynch and Bellew, and names from various traditions in Ireland can be found among administrators and officials, not least that of the Ulsterman, George Macartney, Governor in

1775 of Grenada and Tobago. Nor was it only in the English colonies that such people could be found. An intriguing note in 1781 tells of the presence in Copenhagen of Robert Tuite and Christopher McEvoy, described as wealthy planters in St Croix, and adding that Mr Dungan of Copenhagen also had property on that island.

Soldiers in the service of France and Spain also played a part in the history of these islands. Towards the end of the American War of Independence, for example, several Franco-Irish officers appeared for a time in islands captured from the English, such as Arthur Dillon, governor of St Kitts, and Thomas FitzMaurice, governing in St Eustache. Even more so, Spain employed officers of Irish origin in the islands. The formidable Alexander O'Reilly governed Puerto Rico and, for a while, Louisiana in the later eighteenth century, while another general, Arturo O'Neill, was active in the region in the same period. Likewise, Franco-Irish merchants and Irish merchants based in Spain built trading links in the Carribean area. All this amounts to the barest sketch of a history that has yet to be fully revealed.

It was not the West Indies, however, that was the great destination of Irish emigrant ships as the eighteenth century got under way. Nor was it from the Old Irish or Catholic population that the great majority of the new emigrants was drawn. During the previous century, large numbers of Scottish Presbyterians had moved across into the northern Irish province of Ulster. They had supported King William in the war against the Irish Jacobites but, just as had happened in England, there were remaining tensions between these dissenters and the established church which was supported by royal authority. The result for the Ulster Presbyterians was that they had to endure certain disqualifications and restrictions, and carry burdens such as paying tithes for the upkeep of the established church. When to this was added the raising of rents on the farms which many Presbyterian tenants had taken when they came to Ulster, their eyes began to turn across the ocean to the English colonies in America.

It is likely that it was the economic and related problems and the prospect of a better life in America that motivated the Presbyterians to move rather more than the religious disabilities which began to ease at the very time they started to leave in relatively large numbers. From about the year 1719, and for almost a whole century afterwards, Presbyterians from Ulster formed the major part of a notable movement out of Ireland to North America. This movement was mostly unbroken but there were peak periods in times of bad harvests or rising rents or setbacks in the linen industry. The attractions of America were evident – basically colonies of Protestant culture with much cheap land and opportunity – and the emigrants could leave behind the problems of Ireland where Catholics would gradually press more heavily for the removal of those disabilities still imposed on them.

This migration came to be well organised. Many ships traded between Ireland and the colonies and carried, among other things, flax-seed to the north of Ireland for the linen industry, and had plenty of spare space to carry passengers back across the Atlantic. English navigation laws restricted what could be imported or exported directly out of Ireland but people and food were not on the list. The emerging local newspapers in Ulster became a vehicle for carrying advance advertisements about the ships with the time and cost of their sailing. Agents to deal with bookings established themselves around the province especially in the three main emigration ports – Belfast, Derry/Londonderry and Newry. Other ports such as Larne and Portrush were involved to a lesser extent.

The voyage was long, the ships were small and the conditions often cramped and austere. Sometimes a ship might carry only a dozen passengers and sometimes, later in the century, more than a hundred. There were dangers of shipwreck, smallpox and, thankfully a rare event, starvation. As late as 1773, one ship took seventeen weeks to cross the Atlantic and eighty passengers died. About the same time, another ship made the crossing in less than four weeks, while seven weeks might be thought a reasonable duration. During the wars at the end of the century there was the danger of ships being stopped at sea and young men being seized for naval service. In 1812 there was uproar in Derry over ships being stopped in Lough Foyle and young men carried off to the navy.

The price of the fare fluctuated but there was one way of going without putting money down. Men and even women could go as indentured servants by agreeing to be sold off to a master in America to work for a fixed number of years, if the captain of the ship agreed to transport and feed them on the voyage. Scholars now seem to think that there were fewer indentured servants than was once believed and that more of the northern emigrants paid their own fares, many going in family groups. Because detailed official information about emigrants was often not recorded or not preserved until well into the nineteenth century, there is room for argument about some important features of the whole movement.

This is particularly true in the matter of the very identity of the emigrants. The emigrants who landed in America from Ireland were often described by the people there simply as Irish. This later resulted in truly bitter argument over the question of what contribution the Catholics or the old Irish had made to the creation of the United States. The general view of historians was that there were relatively few Catholic Irish

THE STORY OF IRISH EMIGRATION

in the colonies before independence, and that when people talked about the Irish in the colonies, they meant the Protestant Irish and more specifically the Ulster Presbyterians or Scotch-Irish. This view, however, has been strongly contested by some Irish-American writers.

Most historians today clearly accept that the Presbyterians of Ulster together with some other Protestants from Ireland were the dominant element in the migration at this time. The evidence on both sides of the Atlantic is compelling. What complicates the issue even today are the surprisingly different estimates which leading scholars give of the total number of people, of whatever background, who went to America from Ireland in the eighteenth century. One suggested figure for 1700–76 is no more than about 67,000 while the best guess of another eminent writer is 'perhaps 250,000 to 400,000'. A recent American writer, Marianne Wokeck, has argued that the number of all Irish migrants entering by way of the Philadelphia region was smaller than previous estimates had assumed, and this argument, if sustained, would point to a lower overall total of Irish arriving.

The point at issue is perhaps best illustrated by the argument of David Doyle who puts forward a high figure of apparently more than 325,000 migrants from Ireland in the colonial period but says that 130,000 of these were Irish Catholics. In other words, there were more Presbyterians than some people thought but also more Catholics. He also points out that the Presbyterians coming in family groups and with women as well as men formed settled communities in particular areas, and thus had a continuing impact as a group. The Catholics, being mostly single men, indentured servants or other types of worker, did not form communal settlements, and married American women. They were less visible, and became largely submerged as a group in American society.

This argument will hardly be accepted without much further discussion. What is certain is that the presence of the Ulstermen and other Irish Protestants was remarkable and very visible. After some early movement into New England, the main thrust of these emigrants was into Pennsylvania and the Cumberland valley and then spreading out into Virginia, the Carolinas and Georgia. They were interested in acquiring land and became famous for their hardiness in the frontier areas of the colonies, but that is to enter into American history which cannot be pursued here.

Many remarkable people emerged from this community in a variety of spheres – in business, education and politics. Men such as James Logan who was a chief administrator in Pennsylvania and Charles Thomson who was Secretary of the Continental Congress combined official careers with scholarly achievement. There were leading figures in the Presbyterian church and associated educational work, such as Francis Makemie, Francis Alison and William Tennant, men whose efforts are still recalled. The Dublin Presbyterian George Bryan played a prominent part in the abolition of slavery in Pennsylvania in the later eighteenth century.

The prominent part played by Ulstermen in the movement towards American Independence hardly needs retelling. Several signed the Declaration of Independence and many of the leading generals of the army, of whom perhaps the best remembered are Henry Knox and Richard Montgomery, were drawn from this community, as indeed was a significant portion of the army itself. The list of those of Ulster descent who were prominent in the revolutionary cause is a lengthy one; it would include Thomas McKean of Delaware and Joseph Reed of Pennsylvania and many others. Later descendants of this emigrant community also became notable whether as industrialists or soldiers or, in a number of cases, as Presidents of the United States.

The presence of the older or Catholic Irish in colonial America has also its intriguing side. At one time its seemed as if a negligible number of them could be traced there, but researchers were able to find scattered but persistent examples of old Gaelic or Irish Anglo-Norman names in old registers or army lists. There is the short and often repeated list of Catholic notables such as Charles Carroll, Stephen Moylan, Thomas FitzSimons or Thomas Dongan. Names common in an older Ireland but whose bearers may not now be Catholics turn up in the roll of the first Continental Congress – such as Pierse Long, James Duane, Thomas Burke, Cornelius

Harnett, John Kean and several others. Likewise in the politics of the various colonies one finds a Robert Barnewall and a Daniel Dulany, a Thomas Lynch and an Aedanus Burke. The military names of John Sullivan, John Barry and Thomas Conway are perhaps better known, but it is less well known that many Franco-Irish officers participated in the War of Independence, as did various Irish officers in the Spanish armed services.

The emergence of the new United States did not immediately end the old pattern of Irish emigration. The strongly northern character of the movement to North America could still be seen as late as 1811, and even beyond that there was a strong Ulster and Protestant outflow. With the ending of the Napoleonic Wars in 1815, however, a change could be detected and the signs of a much greater flood began to appear. What was at hand was not just a development or a new phase, but the start of an exodus of literally millions of Irish people. They were about to move in huge numbers to neighbouring Great Britain, to the United States and to what was to become the dominion of Canada.

Substantial numbers would find their way to Australia and, to a lesser degree, to New Zealand and South Africa. This was, in effect, a movement to the English-speaking world, even if there was a small exception in the group that settled in Argentina. For virtually every community in Ireland, emigration was to become a major feature of life.

The scale of the great migration that followed is so large and its episodes and circumstances so varied that it is nearly impossible to describe it well in a short space. Particularly in more recent years, a whole corps of scholars and writers have given their attention to aspects of the story, but while this has greatly increased our knowledge, it has also made plain that some major contentious issues have not yet been laid to rest. One must also say that the story of Irish emigration can often be set in too narrow a context, as if this was a matter that was peculiarly Irish. The Irish may have been the precursors in the great European exodus across the ocean in the nineteenth century, but the population of Europe as a whole was rapidly expanding, and this led in time to tens of millions seeking a new life in the Americas. Along with the Irish went the Germans and the Russians, the Swedes, the Spanish and the Italians and not a few others. Nor has the twentieth century seen a halt in the movement and displacement of peoples; on the contrary, the migrant and the refugee have been high among the constant and characteristic features of the modern world.

The issues that have divided writers and historians of the Irish emigrations are better brought out into the open. The most obvious arises from the fact that at the beginning of the nineteenth century the population of Ireland did not form one single homogenous community. The great majority, over three-quarters of the population, were Roman Catholic and were emerging from a period when the laws of the country had placed various social and political disabilities upon them. The minority of the population were Protestant and were generally conscious of the differences in culture and traditional loyalties between them and the rest of the inhabitants. There were also various people, of whatever faith, who wished to develop a common Irish identity and community, but

Irish family names on French wine labels

The Irish World, an Irish-community newspaper published in Britain

'Outward Bound,' coloured lithograph by Erskine Nicol, mid-19th century
(Courtesy of the National Library of Ireland)

ELOGIO

DEL

EXC.ᴹᴼ SEÑOR D. FELIX O-NEILLE,

Teniente General de los Reales Exércitos, Capitan
General del Reyno de Aragon, Presidente de su Real
Audiencia, Inspector General de Infantería, Consejero
nato del Supremo Consejo de la Guerra , Caballero
Gran Cruz de la Real distinguida Orden de Cárlos III,
Director primero de la Real Sociedad Aragonesa
de Amigos del Pais.

QUE LEYÓ EN LA JUNTA DE 31 DE JULIO DE 1795

EL DOCTOR DON ANTONIO ARTETA ,
Arcediano de Aliaga , Dignidad de la Santa Iglesia Me-
tropolitana de Zaragoza , Consiliario primero de la Real
Academia de San Luis de las Nobles Artes , Sócio de
Número y de Mérito literario de la misma
Sociedad.

CON LICENCIA.

MADRID, EN LA IMPRENTA REAL,

AÑO DE 1796.

Title page of a eulogy written on the death of Irishman Felix O'Neill,
onetime collaborator of Bonnie Prince Charlie and Flora Macdonald,
who afterwards pursued a successful career in the Spanish military. His
credentials listed here include 'Lieutenant General of the Royal Armies,
Captain General of the Kingdom of Aragon . . . Inspector General of
Infantry, Member of the Supreme Council of War, Knight of the
Grand Cross of the Royal Order of Charles III . . . '

Statue of Annie, Anthony and Philip Moore who left Cobh on
20 December 1891 on the SS *Nevada*. Annie was the first among
millions to be admitted to the United States through Ellis Island
(Photo by Pam Coughlan)

Irish-American President John F. Kennedy was enthusiastically
welcomed when he visited Ireland in June 1963. Here he is
seen on Military Road in Cork (*Examiner*)

that was by no means easy, not least because of the implications for relationships with Great Britain. This all led to complications when Irish people went abroad. Sometimes all people from Ireland were labelled as Irish, and sometimes the term 'Irish' was reserved for Irish Catholics, and this was not always meant as a compliment. Some modern scholars, moreover, have argued that the part played by Protestants in the story of Irish emigration has been greatly under-emphasised.

This can become clearer when one looks at the actual course of events. In the early years of the nineteenth century, the population of Ireland continued to soar. The economy of most of the country was based on agriculture, although there were areas of industrial development such as in linen manufacture in the northern province of Ulster and some other enterprises. An ever-increasing number of families lived as tenants and sub-tenants on tiny plots of land producing basic crops, such as potatoes. The reports of observers convey a general picture of poverty and underdevelopment, even if a sympathetic visitor such as the French social philosopher

Alexis de Tocqueville viewed the situation of the majority in a more understanding way than others did.

The return of peace to Europe brought a drop in demand for Irish food, and what with periodic and deadly crop failures and political excitement, there was a huge increase in emigration between 1815 and 1845. Substantial numbers were still leaving from Ulster but now there was a large flow from many other parts of the island. By 1841, there were already over 400,000 people from Ireland in Great Britain and an even greater number in North America. It was not yet the departure of the very poorest, but the great Irish exodus had begun.

Even this great outflow was soon overwhelmed by a disaster. In 1845 and 1846, a disease struck the potato crop on which so many of the peasantry depended. For the following year there was a lack of seed and in 1848-49 the crop failed again. There were at the start more than eight million people in the country and although some regions were much less vulnerable than others, the lives of literally millions were endangered. Hunger and starvation was followed by fever and disease, and it is thought that in 1845-51 perhaps a million people died beyond the normally expected total. Hundreds of thousands who were in a position to do so found places on the boats, going eastwards to Britain and westwards across the Atlantic Ocean. Ireland was experiencing what was known to its people ever afterwards as the Great Famine.

There had long been a supply of sailing ships carrying emigrant passengers to America but now the demand for places led to all kinds of extra hardship. Some ships were wrecked at sea, perhaps forty-five between 1847 and 1852, and some of these were well-remembered disasters. There was the *Exmouth* from Derry/Londonderry sailing in 1847 with a reported 251 passengers for Quebec. It was only at the Western Hebrides when it sank, losing virtually all its passengers. The following year, there was the *Ocean Monarch* which was still in the Liverpool estuary with about 350 passengers when it went ablaze, and despite rescue attempts 176 people died. It was later reported that several thousands of pounds in gold were found on Irish victims, indicating a variety of social conditions among the passengers. And there was a list of survivors including, 'Donaghan, Mary (a child, its mother lost)'.

Two other instances may be mentioned. In 1848 a small steamboat, the *Londonderry*, left Sligo for Liverpool, bringing some 170 passengers, most or all of whom were intending to sail from that port to America. A bad storm developed and a large number of people were pressed into a small area in the forecastle with the entrance blocked. The air supply gave out and passengers were suffocated and trampled. When the ship put in at the port of Derry, it was found that there were seventy-two dead bodies on board. The second instance is one recounted by Terry Coleman and relates to the slightly later date of 1853. It arises from the evidence given by one John Ryan of Limerick to a parliamentary committee in which he described his voyage from Liverpool on the *E.Z.*, apparently not a normal emigrant ship. He was placed with thirteen other people – eight of whom were the Fitzgerald family – on the upper deck in 'a house made with boards over the hatchway.' When John Ryan happened to be outside, the sea struck 'the house' and washed the occupants overboard. The committee asked him: 'Of the Fitzgerald family; how many of them remained alive?' He answered: 'None.' Thus was recorded for history the memory of an obscure and tragic Irish family of the Famine era.

These were minor episodes when compared with the fate of many thousands in the year 1847. For various reasons the passage to what is now Canada was generally cheaper and more accessible, and a procession of ships brought often half-starved and feverish migrants up the St Lawrence river towards Quebec. Quarantine regulations were put in force and the flood of sick and desperate people overwhelmed the arrangements made to deal with them. Including in the total those who died on the voyage and in the quarantine centre at Grosse Ile and the many who succumbed in the hospitals and elsewhere on the mainland, the number of dead is variously computed at over 15,000 or even as many as 17,000. And these were not the only migrants who died that year in and about the ports of Britain and North America.

It is not easy, because of various problems about the completeness of records, to say precisely how many emigrants left Ireland in the nineteenth century. David Fitzpatrick has suggested a figure of some 7.5 million for the period 1815-1914, and the French scholar Jacques Verrière has made a similarly high estimate. Other estimates may put the figure at six million or less, but there is no doubt that the total was huge. We do know that at one point in the century – in the 1870s – more than three million Irish-born people were living outside Ireland, over half of them in the United States and the rest in Britain, Canada, Australia and elsewhere.

Huge numbers poured out during the Famine years, and the yearly total remained very high, with a few intermissions, for the rest of the century. Especially in the earlier phase family groups had left, but a striking feature of the later emigration was the outflow of the young and unmarried, both men and women. Virtually all parts of the country were affected but as the century developed, the western and south-western counties witnessed relatively higher rates of departure.

The state and some landlords arranged schemes and incentives to assist tenants and others to emigrate but this only concerned a minority of those who left, and was particularly relevant to those settling in Australia and Canada. The great source of assistance for Irish wishing to emigrate to North America was the aid sent back across the Atlantic by relatives and friends in the form of passage tickets and money. This was a long-established practice and Maldwyn Jones has claimed that by the 1850s three quarters of the passage fares were prepaid. The loyalty and generosity that lay behind this practice was praised by various contemporaries, but more than one later historian has found it hard to give untarnished credit even for this to the hard-pressed people of the era. One modern scholar has even speculated that the chief reason perhaps for the high fertility of the period was the hope of Irish parents that they would have emigrant children who would send back money to pay the rent and other expenses. How such scheming parents could rear such altruistic children was not explained.

The emigrants of this period poured into the

ports and east-coast cities of North America. They often huddled miserably in slums and shacks and cellars. They commonly worked as labourers and servants, often in the least desired employments. They became a much-discussed feature of New York, Boston, Philadelphia and cities further inland such as Chicago. It was not surprising that there was much resentment at the arrival of such a flood seeking homes and work mostly at the lower end of the labour market. It had to be a shock to the system of a society of predominantly British Protestant culture to witness the arrival in their midst of so many Irish Catholics and so many in a far from prosperous state.

Not all the emigrants, however, remained in the main east-coast cities. Recently scholars have argued that some of them did seek to settle on the land, notably in Canada, the preferred destination for many Irish Protestants and for some Catholics. The more detailed statistical records of early Canada have allowed some interesting investigations to be carried out. Ulster emigrants settled in considerable numbers in Ontario, as did members of smaller Protestant communities such as those from North Tipperary. Some Irish went much further west, and even as early as 1844 the devoutly Catholic Martin Murphy from County Wexford led his large family as a major component on the very first wagon train to go overland into California, which was not yet part of the United States. There the Murphys became ranchers on a large scale.

More typical travellers westwards were the people who worked on the great transport projects of an industrialising America – the Erie Canal or the various railways spreading across the continent. Others went to work in the mines of Pennsylvania or further afield in Montana. A very substantial number of immigrants, perhaps 170,000, were recruited for the deadly Civil War of the 1860s as it spread to various parts of the country. And it was in this mid-century that there was an outburst of hostility and prejudice against the Irish, linked to the Know-Nothing movement which rose and fell as a political force. As the century proceeded, great numbers of immigrants from other European countries were pouring into America, a greater industrialisation was taking place and this inevitably changed the context for the Irish-American community.

There are dangers in trying to describe this Irish-American story under a few simple headings. There are two extreme possibilities when people move in numbers from one land to another. They can all settle together and re-create in considerable measure the kind of society from which they had come and have relatively little to do with other people. Alternatively, they can scatter among the existing inhabitants of the new land, intermarry quickly and adopt the language, customs and system of their new home. It cannot be said that the Irish in America adopted either of these extreme options to any large degree.

The Irish Protestants did at particular times and places settle close to each other and interact together, but they already shared many traditions and values with the existing American or Canadian people. They could be said to be a distinct force who made a distinct contribution but they were not an alien people aloof from the host community. The Catholics who made up the great majority of immigrants from Ireland from the 1840s onwards were in a different position. Scholars still argue as to how deep was the faith and how constant the practice of many of the early immigrants, but it can scarcely be denied that it was around the institutions of the church that many of the immigrants built important parts of their lives and loyalties. They paid for church buildings and later for schools, they associated in parishes, they intermarried to a considerable degree and it was their children who constituted a substantial portion of the American Catholic clergy and religious orders. Men like Cardinal Gibbons of Baltimore, Archbishop Hughes of New York and Archbishop Ireland of St Paul's became influential figures in American life and spokepersons in various ways for their coreligionists. The Irish were not the only Catholics in America but they contributed greatly to the emergence of Catholicism as an important and familiar element in American life. The porters and housemaids of the 1840s had left behind their legacy.

Religion was a controversial matter in nineteenth-century America, and so also was politics.

Many of the Irish were gathered together in insalubrious urban areas, and coming from the land of O'Connell and Young Ireland, they were not unfamiliar with the style of democratic politics and its methods. They entered eagerly into local city politics and frequently defeated the established classes and, often enough, offended men of moderate and principled views. Away from the wards of Boston, New York and Chicago, their descendants moved into the sphere of national American politics. Their collaboration in politics was another way in which the immigrants and their children acted together as a group or community.

There were other spheres in which many of the Irish acted together and one of them, not surprisingly for immigrants who found work in factory, mine or construction site, was the development of workers' associations and unions. The story of the Knights of Labour in America or the Molly Maguires cannot be retold here, but there is a very interesting field of study in examining in the English-speaking world how immigrant workers who retained their traditional religious loyalties took part in labour organisations at the same time as other workers who held to secular socialist values. It is not a simple and uncontroversial story, nor were the Irish by any means the only workers who retained religious links. And many Irish workers did break away from their religious connections. Yet in America, Britain and Australia, the Irish immigrant communities seem to have brought some of their traditional loyalties into the disputed world of labour politics.

It was not only their new lives in America that brought the immigrants together in a shared cause. One of the most remarkable features of the Irish-American community in the nineteenth century, and to some degree in the twentieth, has been the level of support for the homeland of their ancestors. Mention has already been made of the way in which working emigrants saved from their earnings to pay the fares of relatives who could then come to America, or to help out their struggling parents remaining at home. Yet it was public and political causes as well as private ones that attracted the interest and generosity of the Irish in America. Virtually every national cause from the Repeal of the

Union movement of Daniel O'Connell in the 1840s to the independence struggles of 1919-22 attracted organised support campaigns in America and a flow of funds.

The Repeal movement was followed by Young Ireland, several of whose leaders, such as John Mitchel and Thomas Francis Meagher, took refuge in the United States. After Young Ireland came the Fenian movement (later the Irish Republican Brotherhood) which attracted strong support in America. Some Fenians even tried to attack Canada in 1866 and quite a number came from America to Ireland for the small and unsuccessful uprising of the following year. And when a change of direction took place in Ireland with the parliamentary representatives joining forces with the campaigners for land reform, there was massive support for America for the new Land League. American money contributed greatly to the fund established to help tenants who were in distress as a consequence of following the League's policy about rents. Charles Stewart Parnell, the leader of the Irish Parliamentary Party, was invited to address Congress in Washington, and a later leader,

John Redmond, was branded by critics in Britain as the 'Dollar Dictator' because of American support for the Home Rule campaign.

In short, considerable sections of Irish America gave vocal and practical support to Irish nationalist movements often short of resources at home. The unionist minority in Ireland were not short of allies, particularly in Britain, and also in North America, but not quite in the same way. At the end of the nineteenth century, a sizeable proportion of English-speaking Canadians were members of the Orange Order, and many influential circles in the United States were unsympathetic to the Irish nationalist cause. Yet even if Michael Davitt's description of Irish America as the 'avenging angel' was rather too colourful, it was clear that the great exodus of the Famine and later years did have its political consequence.

There was another side to the emigration to America. The migrants had gone to a different society and could not spend all their time dreaming of old Ireland. Their children could make use of the schools and universities that had been created and take up careers that most of their parents could not. They did not live in a wholly Irish cocoon, and marriage with people of other backgrounds became more common. Third and fourth generation descendants of immigrants could claim to inherit more than one set of national traditions, and many would lose touch and even interest in their ethnic background.

More recent studies of Americans of Irish origin, such as those associated with scholars such as Andrew Greeley, have stressed the economic success of descendants of the immigrants – the numbers of successful businessmen with distinctively Irish names, the various political leaders, distinguished writers and members of professions. This is territory where one has to tread carefully as a third or fourth generation Irish-American has been subject to many influences and traditions, and there can be delicate problems in deciding on the nature of achievement. Yet one cannot resist reflecting that this outcome is not what detractors of the nineteenth-century immigrants would have expected.

It seems fair to argue that the great migration

from Ireland showed that people could move to another society and become part of it, but by continuing to hold onto and develop some institutions, traditions and values that they brought with them, they could also contribute to their new society and modify it in some ways. This could happen without being disastrous for all concerned. This has been expressed in another way by the American scholar Marjorie Fallows: 'What the Irish have demonstrated is that America can encompass difference without insisting on eradicating it.'

4

TATIE-HOOKERS AND NAVVIES

It may surprise many people that by far the greatest number of emigrants from Ireland in the twentieth century have gone not to North America but to a destination much nearer to their island home – to no further than the neighbouring island of Great Britain. The very word 'emigration' might even seem excessive for a journey that was often scarcely a hundred miles and sometimes even shorter. Within England itself during the early days of the Industrial Revolution, English people from rural areas could move even greater distances to find work in a growing city. Rural Ireland might have seemed to many just a part of the labour market for British industry.

Ireland, however, was mostly and for various reasons a quite different country to England,

and the change from one environment to the other was great enough for very many people to be described as migrants. Long before the great migrations of the nineteenth century, people had moved between the two islands as visitors, settlers or invaders. The extent of British involvement in Ireland since the 1500s has already been indicated, and in the 1700s there were numbers of poor and working Irish migrants in London. More famous names could also be found, not only of members of the Anglo-Irish aristocracy and military establishment to whom England was a mother-country, but of writers such as Richard Brinsley Sheridan, Oliver Goldsmith and Edmund Burke, of artists such as James Barry and of scholars such as Edmund Malone who had made England their home.

The great movement of the poor and those seeking work and subsistence was already evident in the early part of the nineteenth century. Seasonal workers had come every year from the west coast of Ireland to work on harvests in England and Scotland and return home with some money to support their family or small-holdings. Now by 1841, there were over 400,000

Irish people in Britain who settled particularly in western Scotland, Lancashire and other parts of northern England and down in the growing capital of London. The often depressed and squalid conditions in which they lived attracted official reports and private alarms. On top of this a few years later came the disaster of the Great Famine with literally hundreds of thousands pouring onto the west coast of Britain, some to find a refuge and work, some to die quickly, and some to escape to America. The numbers of Irish in Britain had doubled to over 800,000 by 1861, and they were still found in large numbers in places such as Liverpool and Glasgow, Manchester and London.

Yet these four centres accounted for only about a third of the Irish-born in Britain. There were others in South Wales, in Staffordshire, in Cumberland and Durham. It was the time of growing industry and expanding cities in Britain, of mines and textile mills, of railways, canals and dock labour. The Irish had poured into a country whose population was expanding, and the emigrants themselves were settling down and establishing their own families and thus increasing their immigrant community. But now the number of arrivals from Ireland itself began to slacken off, for it was to North America that most Irish emigrants preferred to go in the later nineteenth century. The 1901 Census in Britain showed that there were only about 630,000 Irish-born inhabitants, and almost half of these were in Scotland. Thirty years later, the total had fallen again to just over half a million, and it might have seemed that the great exodus across the Irish Sea was finally in decline.

This was to reckon without the world upheaval just ahead. The Second World War changed the course of history in Britain with much death and destruction during it and years of reconstruction afterwards. Labour was required for the redevelopment of towns, the building of power stations and motorways and the staffing of factories and hospitals. One reservoir of manpower lay in rural Ireland, and in the twenty years immediately after the war, there was a net emigration from the island of more than three-quarters of a million people. In 1971 there were close on 950,000 Irish-born in Britain, almost all in England itself with this time the heaviest concentration in the London area and the midlands. Most of the immigrants had been relatively young and single and thus many had married and reared their families in their new home. By the 1990s the number of children of Irish-born immigrants was also a feature for social scientists to discuss.

The post-war period has also seen substantial immigration into Britain from the West Indies and the Indian subcontinent and elsewhere. The questions of immigration and the assimilation of migrants became high on the agenda of public discussion. Almost as a by-product of this interest, attention was turned to the most long-lasting and numerous movement into Britain – that from Ireland. It had been notable that unlike in America there was relatively little academic study of the Irish and their community in Britain. There had been a short enough list of relevant studies, but from the 1970s onwards there was an outburst of books and studies on the history and implications of the Irish migration, many of them written by descendants of the immigrants. Some of the themes had a familiar ring.

There was, first of all, a more detailed look

at the history of the Irish migration. The undoubted misery and hard life of the incoming Irish, particularly in the first half of the nineteenth century, had earlier been recorded in many reports and accounts. Their role in the largely unskilled and heavy labour sector of the economy was well documented, and this was often analysed unsympathetically. The worst situations were sometimes presented as the typical. The degree of pauperism and conviction for crime were not infrequently examined in a highly negative way. While it is no business of the historian to whitewash the past, it can be said that today other questions are being asked about the period. A range of studies of different phases and locations of the immigrant community are being carried out in order to avoid falling into easy stereotypes. The conditions under which much of the rest of the British labour force had to operate is obviously one of the issues to be brought into the argument.

The more detailed information available on twentieth-century immigrants has also been used effectively. It has been difficult in the past to make firm conclusions about the integration or assimilation of the children of emigrants into the wider community or about the social mobility of these children. A recent study by Hornsby-Smith and Dale that makes use of detailed and relevant statistical material compares groups of post-war Irish migrants with comparable groups of wholly English background. One result of the study is the suggestion that children of Irish migrants, and especially those from the Republic of Ireland, show a higher degree of social mobility than those from the English control group. Admittedly, it would be unwise to generalise too freely from one study.

Another theme that has attracted recent interest is the role of religion in the immigrant community. A large majority of the Irish immigrants to Britain in the past two centuries have been Roman Catholics and they have entered a country whose adherence to the Reformed or Protestant faiths has been an important part of its history. It would be surprising if this did not cause some problems and misunderstandings. It did so violently at various times and in various places, including Liverpool and Scotland. When this was combined with the low economic and social status of the Irish, friction was to be expected, and this in turn contributed to Irish communities often retaining a sense of identity in adversity.

As in North America, the Irish migrants commonly retained a link with the institutions of the Catholic church. Wherever they went in Britain, they saved money to build churches and contribute to the cost of schools. Priests were attracted from Ireland and later came from the immigrant community itself. Members of religious orders, men and women, were found to operate schools and other institutions. The parish became an important part of life for many, but it is also evident that very many Irish and their children retained little contact with Catholic activities. They commonly sent their children to the Catholic school but left it at that. The result overall was a transformation of the Catholic community in Britain. Before the great immigration from Ireland it had been small and dispersed, if socially and sometimes intellectually distinguished. Now it had emerged as a very visible body with millions of members. It was sometimes suggested in the twentieth century that if all the children of the Irish community and some others had remained Catholics, they would have amounted to five million in number.

There was one way in which this experience of the Irish in Britain differed from that of their countrymen in North America. The Catholic church in Britain was normally administered and governed not by Irish ecclesiastics but by English and Scots. The English and Scots Catholics remembered the tenacity and fidelity of their small community in the days of religious persecution, and they had a keen desire to show to their countrymen that Catholicism was not something foreign and exotic but had long roots in Britain. This would not be easy to maintain if their Church had primarily an Irish face. Thus it was not very common until well into the twentieth century to appoint many bishops of Irish origin, and some bishops in England and Scotland were out of sympathy with various enthusiasms and political sympathies of their flocks. Some modern writers argue that the Catholic schools emphasised Catholic concerns and interests to their pupils but nothing about the Irish background from which the majority of the pupils had come.

The political situation of the immigrants in Britain also differed somewhat from those in America. There was much of the same enthusiasm for Irish political causes as was shown across the Atlantic. O'Connell and Repeal were widely supported. The more militant Fenian brotherhood also had firm supporters such as the young Michael Davitt or the later chronicler of the Irish in Britain, John Denvir. Likewise Parnell and the Land League were given practical support, and the body supporting the Home Rule party, the United Irish League, had some fifty branches in Britain. The Irish were never concentrated enough in British constituencies to elect Home Rule candidates to Westminster, with the solitary exception of T. P. O'Connor in Liverpool, but their votes could not be ignored by the major parties.

These Irish voters were not in the same situation as their countrymen far across the Atlantic. The government under which they lived was the one whose policies in Ireland they commonly criticised. Their children could feel the pressure of being out of step with their neighbours about events in Ireland in which English forces and English administrators were involved. They could expect the charge that their home was in England but that they were constantly disloyal. It was a dilemma that was to recur again and again in the twentieth century. Yet it would be wrong to think that their only political interest was in greater freedom for Ireland. Most of the Irish were working people, and just as the American Irish strongly supported the Democratic Party, the typical Irish voter in England came in time to support the Labour movement and the Labour Party. The presence of the Irish worker was made plain in the Great Dock Strike of the 1890s and later under the leadership of James Sexton in Liverpool.

When the Labour Party seemed to be moving to a policy in 1911 that threatened the Catholic schools, the reaction was so strong that many feared for the unity of the party, and it was decided that the issue be laid aside. The British Labour Party could not easily become a militantly secular socialist party when so many of its loyal supporters were people of religious convictions, both Protestant and Catholic. Likewise in

Scotland, the Irish community commonly supported Irish causes but also gave support to Labour causes. The exact nature of that support has been a subject for recent debate among Scottish historians. Some activists of immigrant background adopted advanced socialist views, but clearly many Scottish voters were able to bring to bear the values of their own background into their work for Labour causes.

The Catholics formed the majority but they were not the only people who crossed over from Ireland. Numbers of Ulster Protestants settled in Scotland and Lancashire, and all over Britain individual Anglo-Irish Protestants took up careers in the army, church or other professions. Names like the Duke of Wellington or Lord Castlereagh from the earlier period are easily remembered or Bernard Shaw, C. S. Lewis, Oscar Wilde or Louis MacNeice from later on. There was also the long succession of military men with Anglo-Irish backgrounds from Lord Roberts to Henry Wilson and Hubert Gough of the First World War or Harold Alexander and Lord Alanbrooke of the Second.

As time went on, both the Irish-born and

their children found their way into spheres of
activity far from the pit, the loom or the parade
ground. The surnames O'Brien, O'Casey, Lavery
or Callaghan could be held by ordinary workers
or by a financier, a playwright, an artist or a
prime minister. The development of an extensive
educational system within Ireland itself meant
that the proportion of emigrants with quali-
fications or professions increased, and there was
a notable flow of people backwards and forwards.
By the late 1990s, the population of the island
of Ireland had increased to about 5.3 million, a
level that had not been reached since the 1870s.
Another turn had been taken in the history of
Ireland and migration.

5

FURTHER SHORES

There are other places besides Great Britain and the United States to which Irish migrants directed themselves in the past two centuries, and while these did not absorb a large proportion of the migration, they form an important part of the whole story. It is true that in 1881 there were about 3.1 million Irish-born people living abroad and perhaps as many as 85 per cent of these lived in the US and Britain. Yet there was a substantial movement to Australia, a colony that Britain was developing at the other end of the world. David Fitzpatrick has estimated that between 1840 and 1914 about a third of a million Irish had gone there, and these were neither the first nor the last of their compatriots to make the journey.

Virtually all the first Irish who went there

arrived as prisoners, the forerunners of some 36,000 who were transported there for offences ranging from stealing linen to rebellion against the crown. The story of their fate was often far from pretty, as Robert Hughes and others have chronicled. Early arrivals included members of the rural secret society, the Defenders, and of the United Irishmen, such as Michael Dwyer and Joseph Holt, who were sentenced after the 1798 rebellion. A small litany of names from Ireland's political history can be found in the convict lists over the years – John Mitchell and William Smith O'Brien of the Young Irelanders of 1848 and John Boyle O'Reilly of the Fenian era.

These prisoners formed only a small proportion of the Irish migrants. A far greater number were given assistance to get there from various state and colonial funds. They came particularly from southern counties such as Clare and Tipperary, with at least some people going from most parts of the country. They were mostly young, many in family groups, and they had to face a long and sometimes unnerving sea journey to get there. They were mostly Catholics, but by no means all; the 1911 census showed that some 26 per cent of the Irish-born then in Australia were Protestant.

Their history was not quite the same as that of their compatriots in North America and Britain. They were mostly young rural people ready to take on the manual and domestic work needed in that new community. They scattered over much of the country, often working in stockrearing and farming. Many did go to the emerging cities but did not usually congregate all together in distinctive Irish areas. They did not seem to get involved in urban politics in the way that happened in Boston and New York. But they were noticeable in trade unions and in labour politics generally.

Once again they drew attention to themselves by their attachment to their religious traditions. All across Australia, Catholic churches and parishes were founded and schools were established. In time a strong link with Ireland was made in the form of priests and bishops and orders of teaching nuns and brothers. Unlike in Britain, the leaders of the Catholic church in Australia were for a lengthy period Irish – in the

shape of such differing personalities as Cardinal
Moran and Archbishop Mannix. Certainly in
the beginning of the century there is evidence
that the majority of Catholics married partners
of the same faith and thus the Catholic community grew in a country with a predominantly
Anglo-Protestant culture.

The historian Patrick O'Farrell has argued
that the Irish in Australia, certainly from the
second half of the nineteenth century onwards,
were not deeply concerned with the political
problems of Ireland itself. They gave important
and generous help to the Land League in the
struggle over its Plan of Campaign, and there
was support for Home Rule. But they now lived
far away and did not form powerful political
associations to assist Irish parties, and 'very few
Irish Australians wanted anything to do with
the Anglo-Irish war.' And with the onset of the
Civil War, 'Ireland', according Professor O'Farrell, 'had become an embarassment to its sons
and daughters.' He considers that by the 1940s
Irish Australia was at an end.

Other scholars may put a gloss on those
views, but it certainly can be accepted that

situations change. People from a whole variety of national backgrounds and cultures have come into Australia within the last fifty years and closer connections are being made with neighbouring Asia. Australians of Irish descent have some very contemporary agendas to confront apart from the historic problems of Ireland. But it is not inevitable that they will entirely forget their history.

Four other areas of Irish emigration in the nineteenth century may simply be mentioned. Some migrants made their way south-eastwards of Australia to the colony of New Zealand and their number reached a total of 46,000 near the end of the century. The population was predominantly English and Scots and Maori, and while the Irish were again not all Catholics, a most visible sign of their presence was the spread of churches, convents and schools in the country. In more recent times, the son of an Irish immigrant became prime minister of New Zealand and an occasional very Gaelic name in the country's celebrated rugby teams is a reminder of an old movement.

It can easily happen that the story of Irish

migration to Canada is presumed to be much the same as of that to the United States. That is not really the case although there are many connections and similarities. Canada was different in that it remained long within the British Empire and developed its own institutions and traditions, and it had within its borders a large French-speaking minority. Its population was much smaller than that of the United States, and so was the number of Irish-born migrants who settled there. In 1881 there were fewer than 190,000 Irish-born in Canada, while in the United States there was ten times that number.

Perhaps the most notable difference was that a high proportion of the immigrants were Protestants, many from Ulster but also some from the other provinces. They settled in the Maritime provinces and Ontario and were particularly strong in Toronto. Initially they had settled on the land in considerable numbers, as also did many of the Catholic migrants. It is possible to follow the progress of these nine-teenth-century settlers because of the fuller information collected in the Canadian censuses about place of origin. Thus in 1940 when there were fewer than 100,000 Irish-born in the country, the census was able to suggest that there almost 1.5 million 'of Irish origin'.

As D. H. Akenson has pointed out, large numbers of Canadians emigrated to the United States and these must have included many of Irish origin. A particular feature of the Canadian story was the long connection between the Newfoundland fisheries and Waterford and the south-east of Ireland. From the eighteenth century, seasonal workers sailed to Newfoundland in their thousands and considerable numbers eventually settled there – where the influence of their accent is still plainly audible.

In South Africa likewise, the number of settlers from Ireland was not very large. A distinguished Ulster Presbyterian, William Porter, played a noted and liberal part in the area's legal history in the nineteenth century. The mining and other developments drew a number of workers there and the Irish, Catholic and Protestant, played a part in the development of the churches in the regions where English speakers settled. As in virtually the whole of Africa south of the Sahara, numbers of Irish people in the twentieth century have spent their lives there as Christian missionaries. These have been migrants with a difference, and their numbers are diminishing, but they will have a place in the record.

The final and unlikely episode to be mentioned concerns a country far outside the English-speaking world. Individual Irish people had found their way to South America not least as soldiers in the Spanish service or British regiments or in the forces fighting for the independence of the continent from Spain. Memorials to an O'Leary or O'Higgins or a Brown can still be found in particular places. But from the 1820s a trickle of Irish people began to make their way to Argentina, perhaps made aware of a need for workers in projects at Buenos Aires. Soon they became involved in sheep farming in land which, it appears, had recently been in Indian territory.

It is not really clear how large this immigrant community became. In the 1840s, a vigorous and enterprising new chaplain to the community arrived from Ireland and he began organising the immigrants. This Fr Anthony Fahy claimed that the community, including the children of immigrants, numbered 30,000 but later writers have calculated a much lower figure. Certainly, numbers of the community became prosperous and a special church, schools and even a hospital were established. It seems that the community kept itself apart with its own institutions. The English language was preserved and a long-lasting newspaper *The Southern Cross* was established.

Patrick McKenna has described a study by Eduardo Coughlan which states that nearly half the migrants came from Westmeath with Wexford and Longford also providing sizeable quotas. For a small community it has provided a number of personalities who have attracted attention, such as the writers William Bulfin and Alfred Duggan and a General Farrell who became President of Argentina.

CONCLUSION

What has been sketched here is merely the outline of an extremely long story. Migration has not been peculiar to the Irish nor has their experience been the most dramatic and harrowing of all the peoples of the world. The Portuguese have been known to say that 'the Lord gave us a small land for our birth but the whole world to die in', and the twentieth century has been a series of huge and continuing migrations. For Ireland the next era may be one of immigration, and it will be timely to remember the emigrant experience of its own people.

It used to be fashionable to say that the one lesson to be learned from history is that people failed to learn from history. There are bound to be conflicting interpretations of the actions and sufferings of the many millions of migrant Irish people, but there are excellent reasons to try to understand them. It is easy to recall the glorious moments and the successful personalities, but a place in memory should also be preserved for the baby Don-

aghan and the Fitzgerald family all lost at sea,
and for many others.

FURTHER READING

Even a short account such as this has to rely on the work of many scholars. The number of books and articles on aspects of Irish emigration has now gone into the thousands. General surveys of the early medieval migrants can be found in older books by authors such as Ludwig Bieler (1947) or in a brilliant if more literary form by Robin Flower in *The Irish Tradition* (1947) or in a book for the general reader by Thomás Ó Fiaich *Irish Cultural Influences in Europe* (1971). Detailed bibliographies of the period can be found in Dáibhí Ó Cróinín *Early Medieval Ireland* (1995) or in James Kenney's monumental *Sources for the Early History of Ireland* (repr. 1966). The illustrations in Róisín Ní Mheara *In Search of Irish Saints* (1994) will be found useful by the traveller mindful of the course of medieval legend. Other relevant works include those by Richard Sharpe (1995) and Brian Lacey (1997).

For the seventeenth and eighteenth centuries, there is now a growing and extensive literature.

For the European continental migration, two recent succinct accounts can be found by Louis Cullen in Nicholas Canny (ed.) *Europeans on the Move* (1994) and by Harman Murtagh in T. Bartlett & K. Jeffrey (ed) *A Military History of Ireland* (1996). Earlier useful accounts include those by J. Silke and J. G. Simms in *A New History of Ireland Vol III* (1978) and *Vol IV* (1986) respectively. A whole series of relevant articles has appeared in the periodical *The Irish Sword*, such as those by Micheline Walsh, Gráinne Henry, Pierre Gouhier, Hector Mac-Donnell and others; and among a range of books one may mention those by R. A. Stradling (1994), F. J. McLynn (1981), T. J. Walsh (1973), Brendan Jennings (1964) and two from older generations, Richard Hayes (1949) and J. C. O'Callaghan (1870).

The 18th century movement to North America has also its own literature such as R. J. Dickson *Ulster Emigration to Colonial America 1718–1785* (1966); A. Lockhart *Some Aspects of Emigration from Ireland to the North American Colonies 1660–1775* (1976); Kerby Miller *Emigrants and Exiles* (1985): David N. Doyle *Ireland,*

Irishmen and Revolutionary America 1760-1820 (1981); M. Wokeck *Irish Immigration to the Delaware Valley before the American Revolution* (1996), and there are other works.

Only a few of the many relevant works on the emigrations of the 19th and 20th centuries can be mentioned. The existence of areas of disagreement and controversy should be noted. David Fitzpatrick provides a brief survey in *Irish Emigration 1801-1921* (1984) and there are articles by Fitzpatrick, David Doyle and Patrick O'Farrell in *A New History of Ireland Vol. V1* (1996). The series of volumes edited by Patrick O'Sullivan *The Irish World Wide* contains many useful articles and one may mention here those by Patrick McKenna and Joseph King in *Volume One* (1992) and by Roger Swift and D. H. Akenson in *Volume Two* (1992) and by Mary Hickman and Bernard Aspinwall in *Volume Five* (1996). Kerby Miller's *Emigrants and Exiles* also covers this period and Marjorie Fallows's *Irish Americans: Identity and Assimilation* (1979) is also noteworthy. From so many others, one can mention those by Terry Coleman (1972), Maldwyn Jones (1976), Lynn

H. Lees (1979) J. A. Jackson (1963) Robert
Hughes (1987) Bruce Elliot (1987) and Steven
Fielding (1993).